WOUl RATHER
BOOK FOR KIDS

Little Monster Publishing

© **Copyright 2019 little monster - all rights reserver**

The content contained within this book may not be reproduced, duplicated,or transmitted without direct written perrmission from the author or the publishe

Little Monster
Would you rather...

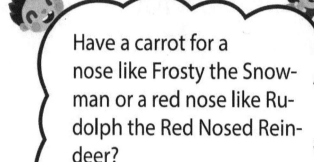

Have a carrot for a nose like Frosty the Snowman or a red nose like Rudolph the Red Nosed Reindeer?

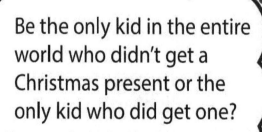

Be the only kid in the entire world who didn't get a Christmas present or the only kid who did get one?

Little Monster
Would you rather...

Be Santa and get stuck in a chimney or be yourself but have to wear a different Christmas sweater every day of the year?

Play in a snowball fight or build a snowman if you could only choose one?

Little Monster
Would you rather...

Peak at your presents before opening them or get one extra present?

Get socks or underwear from your grandparents on Christmas?

Little Monster
Would you rather...

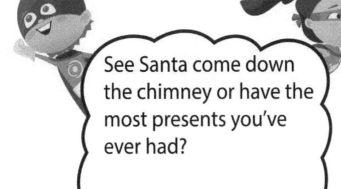

See Santa come down the chimney or have the most presents you've ever had?

Have to wear a beard like Santa for your whole entire life or have the longest hair in the world?

Little Monster
Would you rather...

Get 1,000 dollars or 10 great gifts for Christ-mas?

Ride in the sleigh with Santa or be one of the Reindeer that drives the sleigh?

Little Monster
Would you rather...

Drink hot chocolate or apple cider for all of Christmas Day?

have a frigid Chrismas with lots of snow or a warm Christmas with no snow?

Little Monster
Would you rather...

Be a penguin or a polar bear in Antarctica?

Stick your hand in a freezing bucket of water or have 100 snowballs dumped straight on your head?

Little Monster
Would you rather...

Reside in an igloo or live in Santa's Factory?

Watch Christmas movies all day or go Christmas shopping all day?

Little Monster
Would you rather...

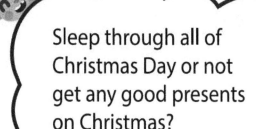

Sleep through all of Christmas Day or not get any good presents on Christmas?

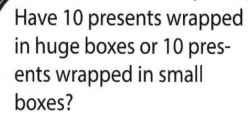

Have 10 presents wrapped in huge boxes or 10 presents wrapped in small boxes?

Little Monster
Would you rather...

Tie a bow around 100 gifts or wrap up 100 gifts?

Go back to the past to your favorite Christmas Day or travel into the future to a random Christmas Day?

Little Monster
Would you rather...

Trade all of your Christmas gifts with your best friend or a random person?

Know exactly what presents you're getting one month before Christmas or have to wait one week after Christmas to open up all of your gifts?

Little Monster
Would you rather...

Spend every Christmas with good friends and family but not have as many presents or get more presents but not have any friends or family?

Have a magic button that made your mom stop talking or a magic button that made your dad stop talking?

Little Monster
Would you rather...

To sing Christmas songs in a church choir or sing them at your school?

Have to shovel snow every day during Christmas break or not have any snow at all?

Little Monster
Would you rather...

Be required to have the bristles of a Christmas tree as your hair or Christmas tree pine cones as your ears?

To write a 10 page essay about Christmas or do 10 pages of math over your Christmas break?

Little Monster
Would you rather...

Be Santa Claus or one of his reindeer?

Eat each of the cookies or drink all of the milk if you were Santa Claus?

Little Monster
Would you rather...

Get coal in your stocking or get no gifts at all?

Have to write down all of the gifts that children wanted or wrap all of the gifts if you were one of Santa's elves?

Little Monster
Would you rather...

Have to wear Christmas lights around your body or have jingle bells attached around your waist?

Have chocolate milk be the only drink that you can have or gingerbread muffins be the only treat that you eat?

Little Monster
Would you rather...

Have to drink gravy instead of water or eat the entire turkey?

Show up to school wearing a Santa Claus outfit or a Grinch outfit?

Little Monster
Would you rather...

Play in one foot of snow or play when there is no snow at all?

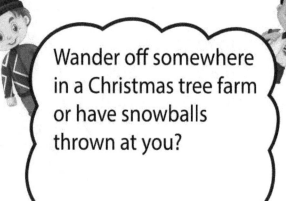

Wander off somewhere in a Christmas tree farm or have snowballs thrown at you?

Little Monster

Would you rather...

Give one gift to someone who doesn't have any gifts or keep 10 gifts for yourself?

Get 10 pieces of candy or 10 small toys in your Christmas stocking?

Little Monster

Would you rather...

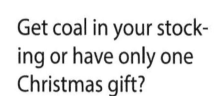

Get coal in your stocking or have only one Christmas gift?

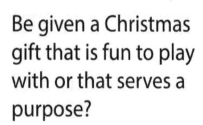

Be given a Christmas gift that is fun to play with or that serves a purpose?

Little Monster
Would you rather...

Have a winter break that is as long as summer break or a summer break that is as short as winter break?

Help make an excellent Christmas meal or help decorate the Christmas tree?

Little Monster

Would you rather...

Have two candy canes or one treat that you could choose every day?

Put up super hero themed Christmas decorations or Disney themed decorations?

Little Monster

Would you rather...

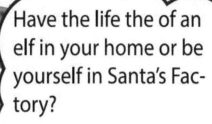

Have the life the of an elf in your home or be yourself in Santa's Factory?

Get the best gift ever but have to give it away or get an okay gift but keep it?

Little Monster

Would you rather...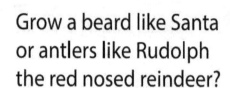

Grow a beard like Santa or antlers like Rudolph the red nosed reindeer?

Play a character in "The Grinch" or "The Search For Santa Paws"?

Little Monster
Would you rather...

Be forced to wear a red nose to school or dress up as the Grinch for one week?

Live with Santa in the North Pole or travel all the way to the South Pole?

Little Monster
Would you rather...

Be best friends with Santa's head elf or with Frosty the Snowman?

Never be able to eat treats again or never celebrate Christmas again?

Little Monster
Would you rather...

Talk like you're singing a Christmas melody or sing like you're talking?

Have five people to celebrate Christmas with or 500 people?

Little Monster
Would you rather...

Be the Grinch who stole Christmas or Scrooge who didn't give anyone presents?

Have a carrot for a nose like Frosty the Snowman or a red nose like Rudolph the Red Nosed Reindeer?

Little Monster

Would you rather...

Be the only kid in the entire world who didn't get a Christmas present or the only kid who did get one?

Be Santa and get stuck in a chimney or be yourself but have to wear a different Christmas sweater every day of the year?

Little Monster
Would you rather...

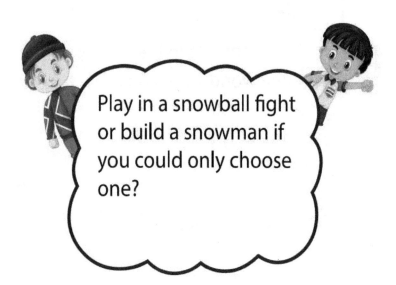

Play in a snowball fight or build a snowman if you could only choose one?

Peak at your presents before opening them or get one extra present?

Little Monster
Would you rather...

Get socks or underwear from your grandparents on Christmas?

See Santa come down the chimney or have the most presents you've ever had?

Little Monster
Would you rather...

Have to wear a beard like Santa for your whole entire life or have the longest hair in the world?

Get 1,000 dollars or 10 great gifts for Christmas?

Little Monster

Would you rather...

Be able to read minds or predict the future?

Ride in the sleigh with Santa or be one of the Reindeer that drives the sleigh?

Little Monster
Would you rather...

Drink hot chocolate or apple cider for all of Christmas Day?

Have a frigid Christmas with lots of snow or a warm Christmas with no snow?

Little Monster
Would you rather...

Be a penguin or a polar bear in Antarctica?

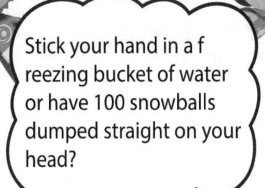

Stick your hand in a freezing bucket of water or have 100 snowballs dumped straight on your head?

Little Monster
Would you rather...

Reside in an igloo or live in Santa's Factory?

Watch Christmas movies all day or go Christmas shopping all day?

Little Monster
Would you rather...

Sleep through all of Christmas Day or not get any good presents on Christmas?

Have 10 presents wrapped in huge boxes or 10 presents wrapped in small boxes?

Little Monster
Would you rather...

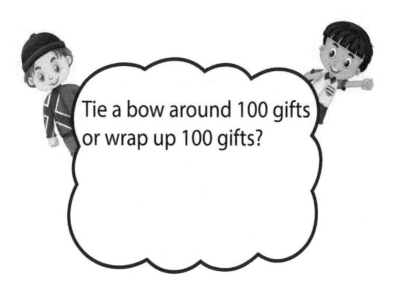

Tie a bow around 100 gifts or wrap up 100 gifts?

Go back to the past to your favorite Christmas Day or travel into the future to a random Christmas Day?

Little Monster
Would you rather...

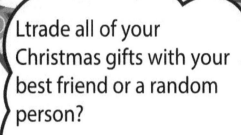

trade all of your Christmas gifts with your best friend or a random person?

know exactly what presents you're getting one month before Christmas or have to wait one week after Christmas to open up all of your gifts?

Little Monster
Would you rather...

Have your room redecorated however you want or ten toys of your choice can be any price?

Spend every Christmas with good friends and family but not have as many presents or get more presents but not have any friends or family?

Little Monster
Would you rather...

Be able to do flips and backflips or break dance?

Everything in your house be one color or every single wall and door be a different color?

Little Monster
Would you rather...

Visit the international space station for a week or stay in an underwater hotel for a week?

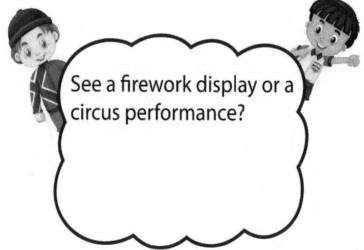

See a firework display or a circus performance?

Little Monster
Would you rather...

Go skiing or go to a water park?

Fly a kite or swing on a swing?

Little Monster
Would you rather...

39. Would you rather only be able to walk on all fours or only be able to walk sideways like a crab?

40. Would you rather start a colony on another planet or be the leader of a small country on Earth?

Little Monster
Would you rather...

41. Would you rather be a wizard or a superhero?

42. Would you rather be able to see things that are very far away, like binoculars or be able to see things very close up, like a microscope?

Little Monster
Would you rather...

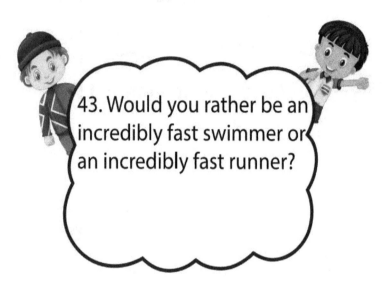

43. Would you rather be an incredibly fast swimmer or an incredibly fast runner?

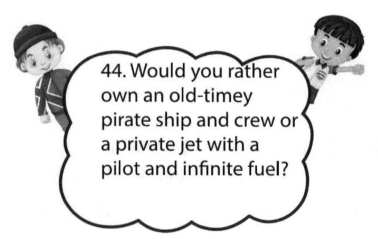

44. Would you rather own an old-timey pirate ship and crew or a private jet with a pilot and infinite fuel?

Little Monster
Would you rather...

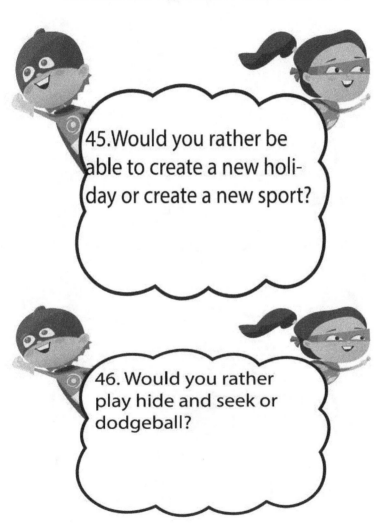

45. Would you rather be able to create a new holiday or create a new sport?

46. Would you rather play hide and seek or dodgeball?

Little Monster
Would you rather...

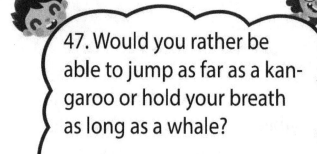

47. Would you rather be able to jump as far as a kangaroo or hold your breath as long as a whale?

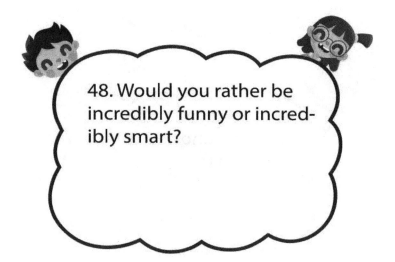

48. Would you rather be incredibly funny or incredibly smart?

Little Monster
Would you rather...

49. Would you rather dance or sing?

50. Would you rather it be warm and raining or cold and snowing today?

Little Monster
Would you rather...

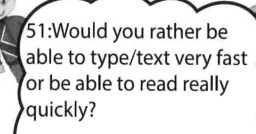

51: Would you rather be able to type/text very fast or be able to read really quickly?

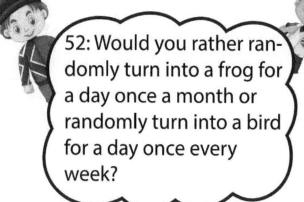

52: Would you rather randomly turn into a frog for a day once a month or randomly turn into a bird for a day once every week?

Little Monster
Would you rather...

47: Would you rather have the chance to design a new toy or create a new TV show?

48: Would you rather be really good at math or really good at sports?

Little Monster
Would you rather...

53: Would you rather be really good at math or really good at sports?

54: Would you rather become five years older or two years younger?

Little Monster
Would you rather...

Have a full suit of armor or a horse?

Be a master at drawing or be an amazing singer?

Little Monster
Would you rather...

Have ninja-like skills or have amazing coding skills in any language?

Be able to control fire or water?

Little Monster
Would you rather...

Have a new silly hat appear in your closet every morning or a new pair of shoes appear in your closet once a week?

Be able to remember everything you've ever seen or heard or be able to perfectly imitate any voice you heard?

Little Monster
Would you rather...

Drink every meal as a smoothie or never be able to eat food that has been cooked?

Meet your favorite celebrity or be on a TV show?

Little Monster
Would you rather...

Sail a boat or ride in a hang glider?

Brush your teeth with soap or drink sour milk?

Little Monster
Would you rather...

Be a famous inventor or a famous writer?

Be a master at origami or a master of sleight of hand magic?

Little Monster
Would you rather...

Have a tail that can't grab things or wings that can't fly?

Have a special room you could fill with as many bubbles as you want, anytime you want or have a slide that goes from your roof to the ground?

Little Monster
Would you rather...

Dance in front of people or sing in front of people?

Ride a very big horse or a very small pony?

Little Monster
Would you rather...

Be able to shrink down to the size of an ant any time you wanted to or be able to grow to the size of a two-story building anytime you wanted to?

Be able to move silently or have an incredibly loud and scary voice?

Little Monster

Would you rather...

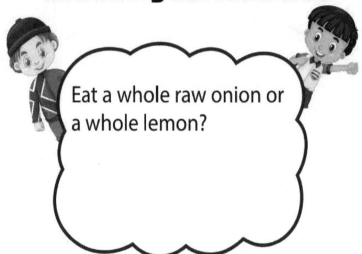

Eat a whole raw onion or a whole lemon?

Be incredibly luck with average intelligence or incredibly smart with average luck?

Little Monster

Would you rather...

Be able to change color to camouflage yourself or grow fifteen feet taller and shrink back down whenever you wanted?

Instantly become a grown up or stay the age you are now for another two years?

Little Monster
Would you rather...

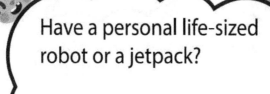

Have a personal life-sized robot or a jetpack?

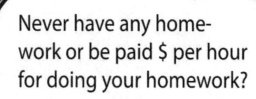

Never have any homework or be paid $ per hour for doing your homework?

Little Monster

Would you rather...

Take a coding class or an art class?

Eat a bowl of spaghetti noodles without sauce or a bowl of spaghetti sauce without noodles?

Little Monster
Would you rather...

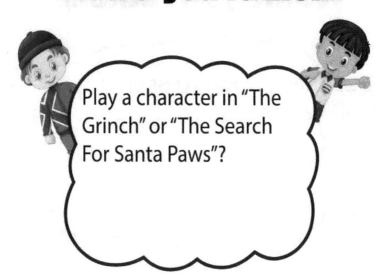

Play a character in "The Grinch" or "The Search For Santa Paws"?

Be forced to wear a red nose to school or dress up as the Grinch for one week?

CPSIA information can be obtained
at www.ICGtesting.com
Printed in the USA
BVHW030223041221
623230BV00005B/379